UNDERNEATH THE POETRY

With

My Girl

Ackeeni Bentinck
And
r. A. bentinck

FyaPublishing
www.randybentinck.com

Underneath the Poetry with *My Girl* / Ackeeni Bentinck and r.A.bentinck.

Dedicated to some of the most exceptional
young ladies I have had the privilege to meet
and grow to love.

Delicia, Haley, Cassidye, Amor, Lakiesa, Ghariesh,
Trinity, Danielle, Dashae, Latiyah, Inae, Zsazsa,
Frances, Kimberly, Delika, Sasha, Jayla, Gabrielle,
Bryanna, Te'ya, Tayla, Havanna, Savanna, Serenity,
Lavonne, Aaliyah, Essence, Maya, Mischa, Tamicia,
Kadicia, Allysha, Doneyah, Ray, Tia, and Kallista.

Thanks for the memories

*I am a princess not because I
have a prince, but because
my father is a king.*

—Anonymous

Underneath the Poetry

Contents

Preface

This is our journey. I have waited for the publication of this book with anticipation from the first day my daughter shared one of her poems with me and suggested to her that we should do a book together. It was like waiting for the day of her birth. She is my first child and only girl. I never thought the day would come when we share a poetic commonality. Our experiences are varied and similar in a multiplicity of ways. Her feminine touch and reality complement my masculinity.

Our outlook and views on society and social and current issues complement and unite us in so many ways. We share the joys, challenges and fears of a parent-child relationship. It is amazing how we find solace and voice using this art form. It's uplifting and refreshing to share this book with you. I am a proud father.

As you grace these pages I know you will be moved, touched and inspired by the thoughts we express using poetry. Enjoy the journey with me and 'My Girl.'

Love Always Daddy.

Womb Conversations

r. A. bentinck

After months of talking to her,

I saw her small footprint appeared

On the surface of Mommy's tummy

For the first time and I was delirious.

"She can hear me!"

She was responding to my questions

With turns and kicks,

And it was electrifying.

It was confirmation that she was hearing

My every word.

Her tiny footprint was magical.

It was one of the ways

She spoke to me.

She seemed to relish the

Sound of my voice

And I enjoyed our daily conversations

From the womb.

Often, she would get so excited

That I got to see pronounced movements-

Was it her head?

Was it her butt?

I was never certain.

All I know it was a large bump-

It was as if she couldn't wait

To see me, she wanted to get out.

 I would burst out laughing

And she seems to be doing the same too.

It was fun for us

But very often painful for mommy,

She would grimace.

I spent countless hours

Conversating with her.

I would call her by her name

And she would respond.

I loved playing with her tiny foot

Every time it appeared on the surface.

We bonded long before I first held her.

She brought me so much joy

During those early and uncertain days of

Fatherhood,

When I questioned my ability

To be a good father often.

And after months of womb conversations

I got to see her for the first time

On that glorious 28th day of January 1995.

And I cradle her softly to my chest and

Gently kissed her feet.

I was overwhelmed by that

Newborn baby smell

That was so heavenly.

After months of conversating

With her in the womb

We both got the chance

To feel each other in the flesh.

I was a daddy with a smile

As wide as the Atlantic Ocean!

The Fatal Fall

Ackeeni Bentinck.

I am haunted every day

By the image of what should have been

your face.

There was a corner in my room

That was set aside for you

Every time I passed by

I died a little more inside

I remember the first time

I felt your touch

It was a moment of bliss, a joyous rush

I remember hearing your heartbeat for

The first time next to mine

And counting your ten fingers and toes

Oh how I loved you so much, though I

Haven't seen your face

But then it all faded away

On that dreadful day

I was laying there face down

Incapacitated, I felt my heart pounding,

Pounding as if it was about to

Leap out of my chest.

I cried for help, but the empty room

Swallowed up my every attempt.

I felt my chest tightened,

My lungs collapsed.

Then there was a warm gush of liquid

Running down my thighs

My body grew cold and

The room pitch black.

When I opened my eyes the first person

I thought of, was you.

I held my tummy, but you weren't there

With much scrutiny,

My eyes searched the room

For my little bundle wrapped in blue

But to my disappointment the only thing I

Saw in blue was a man in scrubs

Then I heard him say,

"I'm so sorry."

Those words immediately created a void,

An emptiness, a huge vacuum!

I wanted to yell, I wanted to scream

But the physical and emotional pain I

Felt were far too surreal

Beneath my breath I cursed,

'Damn you Mother Nature,

You took the life right out of me!'

Twin Tale-Mary's Story

r. A. bentinck

This was no Immaculate Conception,

Mary and her boyfriend was

Just fooling around.

She got pregnant.

The pressure that came with

That realisation was unimaginable.

Hiding from her classmates,

Thinking to herself:

"How would I finish school?"

"What would mum and dad say?"

"How would my boyfriend take the news?"

She didn't know what to do.

To her boyfriend, she broke the news,

But he became a flip-flopping fool

And couldn't make up his mind.

So, she decided one day to visit the doctor.

She said he forcibly evicted the fetus

From her womb and after stuffing it

Into a jar with fluid, he gave her the news.

"They were twins," she said calmly.

I saw the horror on her face

And felt her pain as she grabbed

Her now vacant tummy.

"Twins! Twins! Twins!" she screamed softly.

He tears flowed like torrential rain.

She was feeling pain only a mother

Could understand.

TWINS.

Twins…

Wasn't that her blessing?

Why didn't the doctor advise her or counsel

her?

I sat in her pregnant sadness silently

thinking,

And questions started popping up:

What's the purpose of the Hippocratic Oath?

Did the jar conceal their silent screams?

What does the abortionist do with

These everyday memories?

What was he thinking while staring

Into a young girl's eye?

Does he have a daughter?

It wasn't Immaculate Conception,

But they were twins.

TWINS!

Isn't that some kind of sin?

I am in no position to judge but after all

these

Years I can still recall Mary's story

And for me the pain and sadness

Never fades.

They were twins.

My Unborn Loss

r. A. bentinck

I can never understand why

These memories still slice my heart

Into so many pieces…

Every time!

Now am recollecting:

Spilt hopes and dreams,

Folded premature plans,

A multitude of "what if?" and "how come?"

Scattered on the floor like

Unkept toys

Amidst a bundle of simple yet

Unanswered questions.

I still have the names rich with meanings

And I still visualise faces.

These memories don't take any coaxing

As they awake in the middle of the night

From forgotten cribs.

So here I am again gently rocking;

Spilt hopes and dreams,

Folded premature plans,

A multitude of "what if?" and "how come?"

Scattered on the floor like

Unkept toys

Amidst a bundle of simple

Yet unanswered questions.

They know my face well,

And at times they are

So bold they cry out in public places

And mock my strength and resilience.

So here I am rushing to cradle:

Spilt hopes and dreams,

Folded premature plans,

A multitude of "what if?" and "how come?"

Scattered on the floor like

Unkept toys,

A bundle of simple

Yet unanswered questions,

Diaper pinned to my heart.

Falling to Pieces

Ackeeni Bentinck.

I am falling to pieces!

For this rush of lust

That has overtaken me

Have left me breathless;

Weak in the knees

And though I may be sore and aching

Your smile, your scent,

And your touch I will be craving.

I am falling to pieces!

Every time you call my name

The symphony of your voice

Fills the lucid air

And I become intoxicated as if

I had too much booze.

You have made love to my mind

And now my body only craves you.

The words slither off your silver tongue

And into my ears

A god you must be

Because you make me want to

Sing your praises.

I am falling pieces!

You look into my eyes

And I can feel your strong compulsion,

Compelling me to drink from lust's portion

And I quickly give in to the nefarious notion.

I become your servant and you are my Sire,

For you, I will fulfil all your wicked desires

Even if it means losing myself

To give you all you require.

I am falling to pieces.

My Plea

r. A. bentinck

I am trying baby,

But I am tired of fighting these surging
urges.

I can't conceal them anymore,

I don't want to fight any longer.

You set me afire,

You ignite the fuel in the depths of my soul.

It's the effortless ease in which you carry

Your natural blessings.

It's the electricity in your inviting eyes.

It's the trailing scent of your hypnotising

perfume.

It's your charming and friendly personality.

It's your sensuous simplicity.

Baby, please.

I am counting my lucky stars and

Consulting Shamans

Hoping that I have a fighting chance.

My wilting willpower has grown weary,

And my reliable resistance is getting weaker.

I am tired baby,

Have mercy on me.

Baby please, I am weak.

God Sent

Ackeeni Bentinck.

I am blessed beyond compare

Just when I thought

God has forsaken me

He has proved to me that

He is always there.

There is truly a God that sits

Upon the throne

He has sent me love that

I had never known

He sent me you!

He slowed down my never-ending haste

Set me on the right track

With a different pace.

He has mended all my past

Inevitable heartbreaks.

My heart is no longer on the line,

My love no longer at stake.

I am no longer singing the blues

My heart is at ease, and I feel renewed.

He sent me you!

He has given me someone who

Loves me unconditionally

Someone with whom I can finally be free

Free to be me, make mistakes and

Grow without feeling guilty.

Someone who I can love and

My love will not be in vain,

And who is here to stay,

Forever with me, they will remain

God has perfect timing

And of that I am sure, never denying;

Simply because

He sent me you

Flawed, Faithful and Favoured

r. A. bentinck

She knows the depths of the valleys

And the treacherous step on the rocky path,

But on His name, she still calls,

And His grace still shines through her.

She is flawed, faithful and favoured.

She has survived the piercing

Arrows of the judgmental,

She has survived the harsh words of the nay-

sayers,

The vengefulness of the haters,

The insensitivity of those incapable of

loving;

But His song remains in her heart.

She is flawed, faithful and favoured.

She has been planted by

Fertile rivers and

Her fruits are a symbol

Of her rich blessings.

She has a heart of gold and

Always lend a helping hand.

Her listening ear is comfort for

Many sorrowful hearts,

And His word she imparts as

Wise counselling.

She is flawed, faithful and favoured.

Her sleek and elegant steps are guided,

Her natural beauty refreshes,

An often drab environment,

And leave many men thankful

For the blessing of sight.

She carries a bouquet of gratitude

And strive to be faithful to His word.

      .

She is flawed, faithful and favoured.

She lives her life like a blessing,

She might be full of Flaws,

But she is Faithful to her Faith.

She is Free to be herself because

She knows He died for her.

Taken From Me

Ackeeni Bentinck.

With hands pinned above my head

I heard a buckle loosen, it was pure leather.

My blouse and bra was ripped from my

body,

Allowing my breast to fall free.

He lifted my skirt to my waist

And savagely tugged off

My pure white lace.

I tried to fight, with all my might

But his grip, his hold on me

Was far too tight

I felt his strong, hard manhood

Move sluggishly into me,

And then he began to move

All of the muscles in my body tightened

I cringed at his every thrust

I turned my face and

Gritted my teeth in disgust.

Then he salivated all over my bust

I groaned and moaned not in pleasure

But in pain and disbelief

I thought to myself,

'How could this be happening to me?'

He was just a guy I met on tinder

He was pure caramel, sweet,

Tall and slender

I thought he was a man of high esteem

Never knew he would turn out to be

So wicked and mean.

I invited him to my home

Thought he would have been the one,

But I guess I wasted a whole thought

Because now I'm laying here

Prostrate and numb.

How could I be so weak,

Foolish and dumb?

I succumbed to the harsh reality

And just laid there like a corpse

Allowed him to have his way with me

There was nothing more

I could have done.

Just watch the minutes, that seems like hours,

Passed by and waited until he was

Completely satisfied.

When he was finally finished

He dropped his body on top of mine,

panting

I felt his heart rate slow down

Then he got up, dressed and walked out

I just laid there, unable to move

And I started to cry bitterly

That was the end of me.

I lost all my of my pride and dignity

I was no longer of good use

Permanently damaged,

Scarred and bruised.

Defiled-message from a hurting lover

r. A. bentinck

Rapists you don't know the hurt and pain
You leave in your sordid trail.

He forcibly crushed her tender petals
In her innocent years,
Now am left with all the resulting woes.
Fluctuating emotions, bouts of
Extended depression,
Fragile feelings and buckets of unexplained
tears,
All caused by you!
Rapists you don't know the hurt and pain
You leave after your unspeakable act.

She is a stunning beauty on the outside

But battered and broken on the inside,

Her emotional fortitude has been

compromised.

Abusers, you leave a lot of bruised places

In my love's heart.

There are multitudes of emotional

uncertainty,

My compassion and patients are tested

daily,

I feel deprived of her true essence.

Abusers,

You DON"T KNOW the HURT!

At times my gentleness works like a charm,

On other days my soothing words have the

effects

Of sandpaper being dragged

On the freshly polished floor.

Nothing seems to work anymore.

IT HURTS!

My compassionate embrace doesn't ease her

pain.

I often sit in the company of her pain-filled

silence

And suffer in my masculine way.

Ravagers you don't know

The gaping emotional wounds

You leave for loved ones to see.

This is real.

She is my flower now, and I am committed

To care for her in every way.

The recovery process we take one day at a

time.

They are many rocky days,

And

The emotional work seems never-ending,

But she is my special gem,

And she is worth my

Extra time, love and precious care.

Ravagers, you can

NEVER fathom

The extent of your emotional devastation

Not only

On your victims

But also

The ones who choose to love them

Despite the injuries, you inflicted.

Love has no Colour (For Paul)

Ackeeni Bentinck.

I looked up, and there she was!

With a crown of thick, kinky curls

Biting her plump bottom lip

As she indulges in some

Shakespearean script.

Leaning against the sycamore tree

Enjoying the tranquil summer breeze

That gently blew her dress

Closer to her body.

Appraising her full breast,

Small waist and marvellous hips.

She looked up and caught me staring

Her immaculate pulchritude was so

captivating.

Then she tilted her head and smiled at me

Her smile was as bright as the sun

That nonchalantly kissed her

Dark chocolate skin.

For her, I have a sweet tooth,

Because I love a woman who

Embraces her roots

But if only she knew.

I tried so many times to say, 'hi.'

But I kept wondering what

She might think of me.

After all, I was the one with

The straight black hair,

The peculiar and facetious accent

And the one that wears the dhoti

Our cultures differed in so many ways

But I didn't care. I had to talk to her

And that day had to be today!

I couldn't allow such empress to slip away.

It took some time for me

To gather my thoughts.

I thought of all the right words to say

Then I finally build the courage

I got up and started to approach her

I took deep breaths and tried hard not to

Shake or quiver.

As I got closer, she gazed at me with

Those questionable eyes

I wanted to turn back, run and hide

But I had to be a man, put aside my pride.

As I stood before her, I stretched out my

hands and said,

'Hi.'

She shook my hand in return and replied,

"Hey, you must be the new guy. Jai."

From that very instance

Our love story began.

For her, I would do it all over again

Not caring about what people think or say

About our obvious differences

One thing I know for sure is that

Our love is everlasting.

Despite the social ills and negativity

Eternity, with her I will be spending.

The Sari Princess

r. A. bentinck

All the boys told me the story.

Her daddy has a gun and

Her three brothers

Sharpen cutlass for breakfast

Every morning.

They all drool with admiration

From miles away,

And have become adroit at

Throwing suave words to the wind,

Hoping she will hear them.

Me, I'm an infatuated prisoner and

I cared less about the shackles of fear.

She slowed down as I called out to her.

Her sari flowed with the rhythm of

Her tassa waist.

Her smile glowed like the flames of

Burning incense.

My initial words get muffled

By trepidation that berates

My courageous heart.

Her soothing greetings calmed

My rapid heartbeat that was

Overpowering the noise of the street.

We walked,

We talked,

And shared butterfly glances.

As we leisurely approached her home,

A still small voice screamed,

"ARE YOU CRAZY?!"

And I remembered the story

The boys told.

Her daddy has a gun and

Her three brothers

Sharpen cutlass for breakfast

Every morning.

Dark Place

Ackeeni Bentinck.

It hurts my deepest core

Makes me want to strip away my humanity

So I would no longer have to feel anymore

It slowly shreds my sanity

Bringing to light the darkest

Parts of my soul.

It reminds me of my darkest days

I feel my repeated and continuous pains

That tortures me in so many ways

In ways in which I will never be able to

explain.

I often try to convince myself that

It's just a phase,

But my efforts are forever in vain

Its punishment is far too severe

It recreates my worst nightmares

It suffocates me, weakens me

Until I am stripped of my strength

And unbending stubbornness

It brings me to my knees,

Where I am helpless

And it keeps me there until I beg

And is granted forgiveness.

Caribbean Spice

r. A. bentinck

There is something alluring about

Your quiet exterior.

The coy smile that softly fades away;

Seeping into my being

Acting like an aphrodisiac.

There is a richness in your

Bustling strides as you quickly

Glide by with a teasing smile and twinkling

eyes.

The sleekness of your slender physique

Coupled with your irresistible

Ackee-coloured skin

Makes lusting endearing.

You are like a Classical Jamaican

Reggae love song

On a lover's holiday…

Beres Hammond's:

'No Disturb Sign.'

Or

Bob Marley's:

'Turn Your Lights Down Low.'

Latter

Ackeeni Bentinck.

So we've locked ourselves up in a box!

That limits our strengths

That makes us believe we are

The weaker sex

And creates the image that

Man is superior,

To whom we remain inferior and

Must submit,

Objectified as their sex toys of pleasure

Brainwashed us to believe that

We don't need to work harder

Or we don't need to educate ourselves

Further than high school.

All we need to do is marry some

Doctor or Lawyer.

God forbid if that man leaves us

Today or tomorrow,

What will we have?

Just a bucket full of remorse and sorrow.

It's an awful shame, is it not?

So we've locked ourselves up in a box

A box that tells us we are NOT beautiful

If we don't wear tight skimpy dresses

Or paint our faces with lipsticks and

Colourful powders.

This box makes us believe that the

Melanin of our skin is hideous

And so to be "beautiful."

We set out to change our skin tones

Decolourizing our true immaculate

pulchritude

We have changed the concept of

"BLACK IS BEAUTIFUL"

To "BLEACHED IS BEAUTIFUL."

We have lost our sense of true identity,

We can no longer see that

Beautiful black girl

Behind that yellow veil of flesh.

It's an awful shame, is it not?

So we've locked ourselves up in a box

That tells us we have our rights.

But do we?

If we have our own rights

Then why are we still following the

multitude?

You see,

The crowd is not always right!

Clearly, this box has turned us all into fools

Monkey see monkey do.

Forgive me, I don't mean to be rude.

Yet we tell our young daughters

"To be comfortable in their own skin

And they are beautiful just the way they

are."

While we stand before them

Like true relics hypocrisy,

With our straightened hair and

"On fleek" eyebrows

And "super" clear skin with

"very" black knuckles.

How long will we stay in this box?

It's an awful shame, is it not?

The Good Hair Rat Race
(Curse of the Natural Hair)

r. A. bentinck

I am mourning the loss of another sister

today,

She just succumbed to the 'good hair'

culture.

Her mirror started telling her lies

After tonnes of packaged standards of

Beauty commercials.

Her natural hair is no longer good enough.

She has to get that advertise real Remy stuff.

It's a MUST to meet the 'new' summit of

beauty.

It's tough out there!

She plucked out her eyebrows

For a daily paint job-

One that's long with an elegant feline flow.

Who needs the thick stuff?

It's too…toooo damn disorganised.

While she's at it, she throws in some

Long eyelashes.

She buries her natural beauty

Beneath a thick foundation,

It's smoother and more even-toned.

She can no longer tolerate the sight of

Her naturalness

It's too depressing.

She would rather die than leave home

without

Her false fixes.

It's a crying SHAME!

She is competing in a fast-paced hair rat race

And it's getting harder every day.

The challenges are coming fast and furious:

New 'good hair' styles,

New 'good hair' length,

New 'good hair' colours,

New 'good hair' textures,

Longer more luscious, fuller, false eyelashes,

Hours in the beautician's chair,

The hair stylist now holds

The Holy Grail to beauty.

It's her holy duty.

Thousands of hours consuming

Billboards and commercials

Along with a daily dose

Of societal peer pressure means death to

Her frazzled sense of self-worth.

The gullible and weak

Fall like dried leaves

In high winds.

There is a rapid growth in

Low beauty self-esteem;

So they are supplying a wider variety of

products.

There is fake hair to her every need.

Now there are even fake dreadlocks,

(I can't believe it!)

What the…..F@$K!

Enough!

Gravestone

Ackeeni Bentinck.

I am here, like every year

With the same flowers

Kneeling with my eyes closed

Allowing the memories

Of the times we had shared together

To fill my thoughts

The last time we quarrelled,

The last time we kissed

The last time I made sweet love to you,

Oh, it was a moment filled with

Passion and bliss.

Holding and feeling your soft and slender

body

Against mine,

Chest to chest. Then it all disappeared!

To when the preacher said,

'Ashes to ashes, Dust to dust.'

My heart laments unto this very day

I can't get over the fact that you are gone

But until then I will be here,

Like every year, on your birthday

At your gravestone.

Unpainted Canvas

Ackeeni Bentinck.

Silk words

With a silver tongue

Searching eyes

And wanting arms

Decisive in your every move

Plotting, planning and scheming

Trying hard to put to put on a show

To hide the feeble little boy

Who has been hurt and betrayed.

Maybe once or twice before

Your heart may be saying "yes."

But in your head, that's a "hell no!"

Your silence is equivocal

Never giving anything away

But your actions shout everything

Your lips wouldn't dare to say.

You are like a damaged canvas

Waiting for the right artist

One who will see your true worth,

And will be willing to paint

Despite the many cracks

And years old stains

Until then, you'll have to wait!

New Beginning

Ackeeni Bentinck.

The day is finally here.

The day I have anticipated all my life

Who would have thought,

We would have made it,

Made it thus far in our journey of love.

I inhaled and exhaled incoherently,

As I heard the march began to play.

My father, the main man in my life,

Looked down at me with joy,

A little sorrow

But no regrets in his big, bright,

Brown eyes.

He held my hands tightly as we

Approached the grand opening.

As we got closer, I looked at the door

And said to myself, ' this is it! '

For I knew beyond that door

My new life begins.

It begins with the one I love.

When we entered the grand opening

I could not help but stare at the man

Waiting at the end of the aisle for me.

His eyes danced with joy and love,

As they pierced into mine.

I could not help it, I started to cry.

For joy have overwhelmed me

My father handed me over to the one I will

Become one with.

He held my hands and smiled at me,

Whispering, 'I Love You.'

We exchanged vows and

Solemnly swore before God

To love each other till death do us part.

Our vows were sealed with a kiss

And the announcement of

The new Mister and Mistress.

I knew to myself this was a new beginning

Which meant new blessings, new favours,

New challenges, new consequences,

A new journey altogether

And I am prepared to travel this journey

With the one I love!

To the School Girl in the Video

r. A. bentinck

Not every "I love you" comes

From a mouth that's clean

And a heart that's pure.

Why be another member of this

Ever-growing gullible sex tape cast?

What are your motives for undressing

And having adventurous coitus on camera?

Respect and value your sexuality.

Not every latest fad will elevate

Your teenage soul

And, street creds wouldn't appear on

Your diploma.

You should never be remembered as

The schoolgirl in the viral sex video.

Don't be anyone's fool tool.

Stay in school, learn and apply the rules.

They will help to mould and guide you

Towards the positive.

Your intimate moments should never be

A public box office hit.

Protect and preserve your pride and dignity.

Your virginity and sultriness should be

Treasured and revered,

They should never be the featured

presentation

In a player's home movie.

Beware of the company you keep,

Beware of the books you read,

Beware of visual food you feed your mind.

Respect your sensual blessings.

Wear your school uniform with pride,

Be smarter than your smartphone,

Keep your clothes on in front of the camera.

Some memories don't leave

Like misguided men do

And the psychological scars

Last long after boys grow up to become men.

Red Wine, Red Panties

Ackeeni Bentinck.

For weeks now I've been watching him

From across the room

With his head buried in his phone

I wonder if he even notice me anymore

When I speak, it's like I'm not there

I know he hears me, but is he listening?

But when his little relic of happiness vibrates

His body jolts awake

This man-made gadget has taken my place,

It has become his companion and lover

And so one day when I was tired of bullshit

And while he was in the shower

I got my hammer, grabbed the phone

Off the dresser and I started to pound.

I pound, I pound, and I pound

And as I pound I felt a weight lifted

Adrenaline flooded my body

It was as if I was intoxicated

I was fully aware of what I was doing

But I was unable to stop

He ran out the shower frantically

Pushed me aside aided his phone

Yes, his PHONE!

While I was crying on the bathroom floor

So today I am sipping on

A glass of red wine

With his favourite red panties on

This time he is watching me

From across the room

As though he has lost his mind

With nothing but rage in his eyes

Now that bitch on the other

End of the line is not the only one

That can get his attention

Now his eyes are glued to me

As I lay in the chair with his favourite

Red panties on and sipping on

A glass of red wine.

Panties and Bras

r. A. bentinck

No!

Panties and bras aren't

The only things I see.

They aren't the only things

That enchant me!

I see the strength of a woman and that charms.

I see a robust mother

Loving and caring for her children

And it attracts me.

I see your radiant beauty,

Your childlike mannerisms,

Your blooming smile and

They captivate me.

I see a hardworking, independent

Woman with immense potentials

And it fascinates me.

No.

Panties and bras aren't

The only things that come to mind

When I think of you,

But like your other qualities,

They are alluring too.

Money Trumps Love

Ackeeni Bentinck.

Choose me!

This is my humble plea.

Where was he to catch your tears,

On the nights you cried yourself sleep?

I guess he was at work,

Taxed and too damn busy!

But I was there! Yes me!

Do you remember me?

Please don't tell me you have

Suddenly got amnesia

For I was the one who

Gave you my shoulder.

I was the one who kept you warm,

When you shivered!

Choose me!

This is my humble plea.

Where was he to listen to all your tales?

The good days at your girls or

A bad day of sales

I was the one who always

Gave you a listening ear

I was there! Yes me!

Do you remember me?

When you were down,

And your back was against wall

I was the one that held you up

And gave you support

I didn't have much,

But I still gave you my all.

Choose me!

This is my humble plea

On the nights you needed

Comfort and love

I was the one who fulfilled your

Desires of affection

Where was he to attend to all your needs?

But I was there! Yes me!

Do you remember me?

After many nights of blissful lovemaking

In my arms, you will be laying,

Staring into each other's eyes

Now it's my heart that you are breaking

Choose me!

This is my humble plea.

I see he drives a Benz and lives in a mansion

And he flies on private planes

And jets across the nation

But does he know what is

Your favourite colour?

But I know! Yes me!

Do you remember me?

I guess you don't

Because I am not the one

With the big bank book

I am not the one with

The fancy house or cars

The love we once shared is all gone

I never thought I'd see the day that

MONEY TRUMPS LOVE.

Woman

r. A. bentinck

Her features radiate subtle strength,

She continues to slice

The thick darkness of adversity.

With each birth, she brings hope to a nation.

She cradles a generation in her bosom;

Nurturing it, giving it protection and

strength.

She is a woman of creation.

She has seen a lot,

Lived much,

Survived the gamut!

She is still a woman.

Strong,

Sensuous,

Delicate,

An elevated woman

A determined woman;

She is…

Every Woman.

Woman to Woman

Ackeeni Bentinck.

So you've come to take what's mine.

Did you honestly think that

I would just step aside

And allow you to do what you like?

Without putting up a fight?

Clearly, you have lost your mind!

You walk into my presence

And you start swearing and

Calling me names

So I simply allow you to perform,

Here is a stage

For I see your desperation for

A little attention and fame

You better thank the heavens that

The beast within me is tame

I am astounded by your relentless efforts

Fighting for something that

May never be yours

Your superciliousness is amusing

It has blinded you from seeing

The fight you are losing

Be careful not to step to me,

Because your fate, you'll be choosing

You see, I'm all about lifting

My fellow sisters up

But there are boundaries

If you cross the line

I will f**k you up.

However, you are clearly irrelevant

You are not worthy of my time

Allow me to go back to making my money

I'm doing what I have to do

To get what is mine.

You see, the man you are

Ranting and raving for

He is not my source of income,

Based on your despicable behaviour,

I assume that he is yours!

So you have a right to secure your hustle

But why give this man so much power?

We women were born to conquer

Woman to woman,

Baby girl you deserve better.

Empty Plate-AIDS Orphan Awareness

r. A. bentinck

So here I sit

With my empty family plate

AIDS has eaten my portion.

I'm now malnourished

Because of my lack of family nutrients.

No mum...

No dad.

"Where is my next meal coming from?"

I don't know!

In the meantime,

I suckle on the salty nutrients

Of

My tears that flow abundantly.

Think-AIDS Orphan Awareness

r. A. bentinck

Project your humane flashlight

On the orphans

Search the soul of a child,

Search the souls of these children

Who have been abducted

Into orphan-hood by AIDS.

A once loving nuclear family

Now stripped to shreds-

No mother!

No father!

Youthful innocence shocked

Into an alien existence.

CONFUSED!

CLUELESS!

KICKED into a HARSH

And unforgiving adult reality-

The new role of:

Breadwinner,

Caretaker,

Homemaker,

Nurturer of self and family.

Advance your human faculty,

Shine your flashlight-

Now, do you see a snippet

Of the austere orphan reality?

Justify

r. A. bentinck

Why should I justify?

Justify my love.

Justify my silence.

Justify my faith.

Justify my belief.

Justify my confidence.

Justify my optimism.

Justify my happiness.

Justify my sadness.

Justify my rights.

Justify my wrongs.

Justify my strengths.

Justify my weaknesses.

Justify my trust in the Almighty.

Why should I justify?

The Pondering Father

r. A. bentinck

I haven't always been the best of fathers,

And I have missed some crucial moments

In her life.

They often make me wonder,

    What is she thinking?

I haven't always delivered on my promises

And I know she sits and wish for

Many more things,

It makes me often sit and wonder,

    What is she thinking?

I have spoilt her in many ways

To make up for missed days.

I haven't always been the best of examples

Still, I often wonder,

      What is she thinking?

As the years go by and I assessed my

Performance as her father

I have had to face all my fears

Shortcomings, misgivings and

Be honest with where and how

I have treated her,

Then I sit and wonder

      What is she thinking?

I was never always perfect but

This fatherhood thing

Has never been a stroll in the park.

But amidst it all, I have had my good

moments

And hope it's enough to guide her

Positively in the future.

But I can't help but wonder,

> Have I been a good father to her?

I am Proud of Her

r. A. bentinck

I have never had any known reason to hang

My head in shame.

Amidst a plethora of teenage and young

Adult challenges she has carried herself

Like the graceful princess, she is.

She comes with her own challenges but

I am happy I have never had to deal with

Sex tapes, viral videos, alcohol

And smoking addiction.

She mirrors me in so many

Conscious and unconscious

But is prudent enough not to repeat some

Of my inglorious missteps.

I am proud of her not just because she

Has avoided some prevalent

Teenage traps but

When she faced her own challenges

She had a mind of her own while making

her

Decisions even if they weren't always

popular.

As her father, I have demanded a lot

Of and from her.

It hasn't always been within reason

But she has done enough

To make me confident of being

A proud father.

My Chains

r. A. bentinck

I made the chains that bound me

Disgracing my ancestral memories

I bought into their deceptions and greed

I followed in the oppressors' footsteps and

lies

While I swallow my pride.

I carried the chains that shackled me

Disgracing my ancestral story

I sold my soul into this modern slavery

Chasing their make-believe success dreams

I padlock the *chains* that chained me

I am complicit in my mental slavery

The voices of my ancestors

Call out to me;

I can hear the words of Garvey

Ringing in my ears;

"A people without knowledge of their past

history,

origin and culture is like a tree without

roots."

I can hear Marley lyrical admonishment,

"…we've been troddin' on the winepress

much too long;

Rebel, rebel!"

I can hear Malcolm in his militancy…

"by-any-means-necessary."

I – WILL - FREE - ME!

I have unchained my chains that chained

me.

Dear Daughter

Ackeeni Bentinck.

My dearest daughter

For the past three nights

I have been listening to you cry

Many nights you have cried yourself to sleep

Hugging tightly; your pillow, bear and sheet

Over some boy, you have met down the

street

My dearest daughter

Do not be in such a rush to fall in love

This is not the end of the world

You may encounter countless failed

relationships

And numerous heartbreaks

Before finding 'The One.'

My Dearest Daughter

Dry the tears from your eyes

I really do miss your smile

Do not deprive yourself of happiness

Just because of some guy.

Unwrap yourself from the darkness

And let your loveliness shine

My dearest daughter

Do not be so harsh and cruel

To yourself my love, you have done nothing

wrong

It is not your fault. He is the fool

For he has lost the most exquisite jewel

My dearest daughter

Know that I love you

And to me, you mean the world

You will forever be my princess,

my little girl

And I promise to be there for you

Through all the heart breaks

He's Gone

Ackeeni Bentinck.

I replay the day that you walked through the
door

Over and over again in my head.

I still wake up to stretch forth my hands

Hoping that you are laying on the other side

Of the bed

But all I feel is the coldness instead.

I sit at the table staring at the chair

You used to sit in,

Reminiscing about the mornings we spent

laughing

Then I succumb to my tears,

Now I am weakened.

The silence has become so frightening

And the thought of you is so suffocating

Sometimes I wish I can turn back

The hands of time to when I was yours,

And you were mine.

But all I have left of you are memories,

A trail of pain that you have left behind

And a bucket of tears left to cry.

Mere words cannot express my anguish

When I stare at your picture.

The thought of you is just torture

I thought we had a lifetime together

But now, you are gone forever!

If You See Her

r. A. bentinck

She took the golden rays

Of the sun when she

Left that day.

    If you see her

Don't tell her

I never forgot those memories.

Her silly smile,

Those long walks,

The teary moment,

And the luxury of her company.

She took pieces of my heart

When she left,

But if you see her

Don't tell her that my heart

Is still broken.

Don't tell her that

At night I sit in the company

Of her memories,

And the rose tree she planted

Still blooms outside the window.

When she walked out

She took some of the best of me,

But if you see her don't tell her

That you can still see

The tracks of my tears,

And you can still see the pain

In my eyes at the mention of her name.

If you ever see her

Please don't tell her I have

A book filled with her memories

And the words still come alive

From the tip of my pen.

Extraordinary Woman

r. A. bentinck

It's the endearing image

That s left in the mind

As you swiftly glide by...

It's the piercing softness

In your innocent touch

That sends blood galloping

Through agitated veins...

It's the comforting ease of your presence

That teases the facilities

And fertilises a winged mind...

It's the tenderness in your smile

That grips softly wild desires

In a comforting embrace...

It's the way you define femininity

With such gracile ease...

It's the lingering fire

Of playful desires

That burns slow but

Last long after you leave.

Frangipani at Night

r. A. bentinck

In the sweltering midday sun, they are
dormant,

With petals drooping under the constant
heat;

With a whiff of fragrance here,

And a whiff of scent there.

But at nighttime, it's a fragrance frenzy.

In the tranquillity and the cool of the
evening

White Frangipani aroma dominates the night
space.

There is something in the evening's
atmosphere

That ignites a burst of intense Jasmine

perfume.

It's rejuvenating to the senses,

It elevates the spirit,

Brings back fond memories,

And delivers comfort to my jaded soul.

He that Findeth a Wife

Ackeeni Bentinck.

I woke up, and I thought it was all a dream,

But there she was laying right beside me.

Fast asleep, relaxed and peaceful;

My God, she looked so beautiful.

I have waited so long for this day,

The day I could wake up and stare at her

face

For as long as I want without hearing her

say,

"I got to go home now, it's getting late."

Because now she is here stay.

I pulled her closer to my body

And I inhaled her splendid aroma.

I ran my fingers through her unkempt hair

And I trailed my fingers across her face

I planted a light kiss on her forehead

Then she opened up her beautiful eyes and

Looked up at me

And she said, "Good morning dear."

That was the best set of words any man

could hear

Especially coming from the woman

You loved beyond compare.

I smiled with uncontainable joy

I had to pinch myself for this seemed so

surreal

I have finally found my Queen,

The woman of my dreams.

Exhaled

Ackeeni Bentinck.

I stood over his body,

Pulsating and panting for breath.

I watched him until he bled out.

I watched him as he took his last breath

He was the man I loved with all my heart

and soul,

But he was no more.

Yes! I stabbed him to death.

I dropped the knife

Then I took a deep breath

And EXHALED.

A sudden weight was lifted

I finally felt unrestricted and relieved

No more torturous days of interminable

therapy

I felt so good that I started to laugh.

I laughed, I laughed and laughed.

I screamed, and I shouted

With undeniable joy like a trumpet.

Then I left.

I closed the door behind me

Never looking back to that which held me

captive.

For I knew that was the end

The end to the many sleepless nights and

teary eyes

The end to the countless blows he dealt me.

The end to the many slaps,

Kicks and punches

It was the end indeed

I said farewell to my anguish and misery.

Break the Scale

Ackeeni Bentinck.

I used to see the way you looked at me.

You turned up your nose in disdain

When I walked by,

Like I was a pile of trash in your eyes.

You called me cow, whale and clumsy.

You never took me out because

You were ashamed of me.

Yes, over the years I have gained some

pounds,

Because I eat when I am depressed

And that's what happens when you are

Dealing with a clown.

So to please you, I tried to change my life

around.

I started walking, skipping and jogging

But then you made a fool out of me.

You told me to stop what I am doing,

Because nothing was changing.

You told me I was not good enough

Told me I was too fat,

You dealt with me really rough

And about my feelings,

You just did not give a f**k.

I used to be the victim

Of your punitive and obnoxious criticism.

Damn!

Your insolence really got to me,

But however, I do not need your apology.

Now I have a good man who loves me

He sees all the qualities you didn't see

He loves me with all my imperfections,

Every part of me.

He is my coach, my guide, the real team

player

And every day I am growing stronger and

better.

He reminds of how blessed I am,

Yes, BLESSED!

I am blessed with both

QUALITY and QUANTITY

I am a woman pride, strength, wisdom,

Integrity and dignity,

With thick thighs, a muffin top

And all the extra meat.

I stand tall and proud

For I was created to stand out in a crowd.

So excuse while I fix my crown

Because I am still a QUEEN

Despite the numbers on the scale.

Make way and watch me step out and

'SLAY.'

Now you see me doing well,

You want to step to me

Get all up in your feelings and say

How much you miss me

For your idiocy, I really do not have the time

I was always a diamond,

You just failed to put in some work

To help me shine.

Step aside and allow me to get the love

And the life that is mine.

You had your chance, BOY

BYE!

Belle Jeune Femme (for Haley)

r. A. bentinck

Demoiselle,

I watched you grow over the years

And my, oh my,

What a fabulous young lady you

Are turning out to be.

As you journey through life

Do not be too naïve.

Trouble sometimes knock on your heart's

door

With fancy suits and polished accents.

Dangers are sometimes the shiniest of

objects

That everyone praises and craves.

Beware of the cupids with poison arrows.

Be careful of the vultures

Who take aim at your dreams.

Be watchful!

Watch out for the carnivores who

Only seek after your tender meat,

They often come in clever disguise.

I see your wings are now strong enough

To fly on your own;

Soar high with attentive and alert eagle eyes.

Do not be complacent!

Careless Eagles end up with

Broken Wings.

Your thoughts are your only limitations,

Nurture them,

Protect them,

Fertilise them.

Take time to strengthen your mind

For the battlefields, you will walk

Through.

Cradle your health and beauty,

Always cherish them.

Your natural beauty is worth

More than an advertised brand product.

Choose your company wisely,

Friends are influences.

Demoiselle, a bright future awaits you

Live your life to its fullest.

Bien Vivre.

Best Friends
(for Delicia and Ghariesh)

r. A. bentinck

I do not have enough space in my heart

To store the huge bundles of joy

The two of you brought me.

As best friends, you came packaged

With double the joy and

Double the mischief.

Dull teaching days you brightened

And spontaneous moments of

Laughter and fun you came bearing.

Your level of compassion and willingness to

Learn was a teacher's dream.

I swear you girls have music pulsing

In your veins.

Always with ready dancing feet

And creativity that surprises.

You painted the stage with passion and love.

As best friends, you came packaged

With double the joy and

Double the mischief.

As your graduation day swiftly

Approaches.

I sit in quiet reflection as I count the

Blessings you both brought me,

And with gratitude I say,

"Thank you, Baby J and Ghariesh

For all the indelible memories."

Change is inevitable but

Your memories are everlasting.

As best friends, you came packaged

With double the joy and

Double the mischief.

Thanks for all the joys in a bundle.

Coloured Education

Ackeeni Bentinck.

"Why should a child be deprived the right to
shine

Just because his skin colour doesn't

Matches mine?"

I wish some superiors would

Ask themselves this question

And offer a direct and honest response

Without hesitation.

Why should our children of colour

Be deprived of a QUALITY education?

If youths are the future generation,

Why try to suffocate their growth

And starve our nation?

Let the coloured children speak

Listen to the message of their speech

Hear the tone of their strong voice.

They say equal rights and justice for all,

But are they living what they preach?

Why is it so hard for some people

To see a black man strive?

Why is it when a child has topped his class,

Why ask whether it's an Indian or black

child.

Does it matter? Does it really matter?

Children ought to be treated equally.

Each child has the right to express

Their own unique personality

No matter the colour of their skin or

ethnicity.

How?

Ackeeni Bentinck.

How did this happen so soon?

I needed more time!

An extra minute, hour, day, week, month or year

I thought I had all the time in the world,

I thought I had nothing to lose.

Now that she is gone, what do I do?

This is my question for you.

How do I put all the broken pieces back together,

When there is no glue to hold it together anymore?

How do you convince your heart to stop

aching,

Because the one you love is no more?

How will I be able to do this all on my own?

I am not used to being alone.

She taught me many things,

But she never taught me how to live without

her.

So tell me now, how do I live without

My best friend, my lover?

It's been fifty years

This year was our golden year.

Fifty years of the good, bad and ugly

Fifty years of shared tears, happiness and

love

And we did it all unselfishly.

So how do I live without her?

Please, tell me?

How?

Memories of Mommy

r. A. bentinck

In the tranquillity of my room

On this bright and sunny day

They suddenly erupted,

A gush of memories of my mother.

My peaceful mindset quickly disappears

And I am strangled by powerful emotions.

My eyes are blinded as they drown in

A tsunami of tears.

My room is now crowded with

A plethora of her delicious memories.

Am swimming to survive these

   Memories of mommy.

I have crossed many rivers

And negotiated a multitude of life's perils

But the memories of my mother

Feel like am swimming upstream.

She taught me a lot:

She showed me how to love,

She taught me how to be tough,

But I can't remember a lesson

On how to deal with her memories.

Am struggling to survive these

Memories of mommy.

I stand in the middle of my room

Now flooded with these memories:

The joyful sounds of family time

Ring in my ears,

I can smell the deliciousness of her kitchen,

I can hear her melodious singing voice

Lightening up the atmosphere,

I can feel her warm embrace.

They all use to make me smile but today

Am a drowning man trying to clutch

at my sanity, as I am being carried away by

these unbearable

    Memories of mommy.

Moment of Impact

Ackeeni Bentinck.

I remember seeing her for the first time

After six long years.

Happiness flooded my body,

Tears streamed down my cheeks

And as I approached her

She looked up at me with those pretty

brown eyes

I wiped my tears, and I thought to myself,

'I can't let her see me like this.'

When I was close enough, I stopped

And said, 'Hi!' she stared at me for a long

minute

With her penetrating and questionable eyes

I thought she recognised me

But then she replied,

'My mommy told me not to speak to

strangers.'

Then she ran away.

That was the moment of impact.

The flood of joy turned into a tsunami of

pain

I literally felt my heart break into a million

pieces

As she ran into the arms of another woman

Whom I presumed she calls 'Mommy.'

The woman looked at me and shook her

head 'no.'

And my heart broke a little more

It crushed my heart to know,

That my little girl doesn't know who I am

But it's not her fault, I am the one to be
blamed

I am the one who gave her up

Out of disdain and shame.

I thought it was the right thing to do at that
time

But now I realise that I had given up

The only thing that was truly mine.

At that very instance, I wanted to fight for
my baby

But at the same time,

I didn't want her to be unhappy

And caught in the web of life's

Chaos and catastrophes.

So I had to let go and just let her be

For her happiness is all that matters to me.

Always, My Mama

r. A. bentinck

It was the comfort of

Her Womb

That provided me

With nine months of

Priceless security and loving nurturing.

From the beginning

It was always a Mama,

My Mama.

In those vulnerable

And susceptible years,

She provided me with

Unconditional love and tender care.

Through my early years

It was always a Mama,

My Mama.

In the spring of my

Teenage years

She was always there

To guide and direct me

With firm yet gentle hands

And reassuring words of

Wisdom and indescribable love.

In those vital years

My Mama was always there.

In my grown and rebellious years

When her advice sometimes

Conflict and pain.

Despite my stubborn ways

It was my Mama who

Continued to care.

As I grew older and wiser

It's becoming more apparent

That my Mama will always be here.

Her memories,

Her wisdom,

Her traditions,

Her unique love,

In so many ways

Despite the departed years,

It's still always my Mama

Who often guide and direct

My ways.

Just like my beginning

It's still always my Mama

In so many ways.

Conversations with a Young Girl

r.A. bentinck

She is a natural beauty

In so many ways,

But

All that flows from her mouth

Is self-hatred.

How do you talk to a young girl

Who cannot see her value and self-worth?

She still has her angelic

Newborn eyes

And a smile that glows with joy

But the words that emanate

From her mouth

Are like a dagger

To her tender heart.

How do you talk to a young girl

Who cannot see her natural beauty?

Society's standard is all she knows

And her naturalness

Her mirror keeps rejecting.

She feels neglected,

Unloved,

Hated,

Discarded.

Her complexion is too chocolate,

Her hair too kinky and unruly,

She just doesn't fit in.

How do you convince a young girl

That her uniqueness is a gorgeous blessing?

There is no hatred

Like self-hatred,

And she has a surplus of this stuff.

My heart bleeds for her,

My logical arguments

And sensible reasoning

Is not penetrating the fortress of her

Made up mind-

"I'm not pretty!"

She keeps reminding me

For the umpteenth time.

My persuasive bank account

In now bankrupt on her.

How do you talk to a young girl

Who cannot see her value and self-worth?

Can someone tell me,

Please?

The Modern Girl's 23rd Psalm

r.A. bentinck

As long as society is her Shepherd

She shall always want.

They will always make her lie

In green pastures for promiscuous

And commercial gains.

She will be led in paths of unrighteousness

In the name of fame, fashion and

Material gains.

Yes, there will always be valleys, shadowy

Places, death and destruction.

Evil will she always fear for

The rest of her days-

The Creator will be the furthest

From her mind.

Their rod and staff will not

Provide divine comfort

In her times of spiritual need.

They will feast at her table

For all to see.

Trials and tribulations will

Anoint her head-

And her stress cup will

Always runneth over.

Surely perils and heartaches

Shall follow her all the days

Of her life:

And she will dwell in their

House of indoctrination and manipulation

Forever and ever.

Amen.

Nymphomania

Ackeeni Bentinck.

Her back arched as if it's an exorcism

Gasping for air,

As though she is suffocating

Viciously gripping the fabric beneath her

Her body starts convulsing

Which was followed by a timely explosion

She then lay there, almost lifeless

Breathing still ragged,

She folded up like a white lotus

Her heart began to bleed

As she closed her eyes

And allowed her mind to wonder

Blocking out her present reality

Praying silently that it all might be a dream

For she has succumbed to yet another

temptation

All in the name of feeling that one single

Moment of 'HIGH.'

To feel that hard and throbbing flesh

Between her thighs

She just couldn't seem to stop

No matter how hard she tries

But she was growing weary of the multiple

Compulsive self-stimulation,

The cybersex and the pornography.

She swore this time was the last time,

Just like she swore the last time.

The Sheet's Secrets

r. A. bentinck

If sheets had eyes,

How would they see us?

Would they see actors,

With contorted faces?

Helpless carnal prisoners?

Or would they see victims of

Blistering emotions?

If sheets could speak,

What would they say

To us?

About us?

Would they say we are

Creating indescribable memories?

Would these sheets spill our secret?

If these sheets could feel

Would they scream out under

The intensity?

Would the heat from bodies tossing,

And turning burn?

Would these sheets be hurt?

If sheets were neat freaks

Would they fret and fuss?

A lot?

Over their now crumpled state,

Created by our

Sensitive insensitivities?

If these sheets knew our names

Would they call us out?

Saying:

Slow down,

Calm down,

Just relax!

Would they complain

About being drenched?

My Dearest Son

Ackeeni Bentinck.

My dearest son,

Though your father is not around,

Let that not be your excuse

For not becoming the great man

You are destined to be.

Be the difference we want to see in this

society

My dearest son,

Though I am your mother,

I am a woman too

And just as you respect me,

You must respect all women too.

Never debase a woman

Even if she seems unworthy

If you have nothing positive to say

Keep a still tongue.

My dearest son,

When you're older and have found

The woman you love,

Never raise your hand or lay a finger upon
her

Unless it is to pamper and pleasure her.

She is not a punching bag.

She is your companion, soulmate and lover.

My dearest son,

When you have your children of your own

Love them with all your might

And be there for them always

Do not only be PRESENT,

But let your PRESENCE be felt.

Give them what your father did not give to

you.

My dearest son,

Though there are many ills in this society,

You will find your right path

But I do not promise you it will be easy.

Just remember to keep your head high

And be the great man

You are destined to be.

Someday-Ms Impatient

r. A. bentinck

Someday,

A young man will get lost

Just looking into your eyes.

Someday,

A young man will sing

To the heavens just

Because he found your love.

Someday,

A young man will have the

Privilege to sit in the company

Of your smile.

Someday,

One sensible young man will treat you

Like the queen you are-

Just like royalty.

> Someday,

You will come to realise

Your true value,

And you will never settle for

Anything but the best.

> Someday,

Your garden will bloom

With beautiful roses

And the rain will fall just for you.

> Someday,

You will find a way

To smile through the pouring rain.

> Someday,

It will all get easier.

> Someday,

It will all make sense.

    Someday,

You will have the answers

To the difficult questions

    And the solutions

To the unsolvable problems.

    Someday.

Just be patient.

An Open Letter to a Father
(for Jade)

r. A. bentinck

Dear Father,

Have you seen your daughter lately?

You are missing a lot.

You have missed a gamut of her cuteness.

I see her daily in my classroom,

And she is growing into a wonderful young
lady.

She is smart,

She is extremely pretty,

Her hugs are rich with I love you,

She is witty and perceptive,

And most of all, she is loving.

I have never seen your face,

But I see you in her eyes.

Have you seen her smile lately?

It's heartwarming.

Your absence and missteps have

Turned parts of her heart to concrete.

Father, reach out to your baby girl.

Her glowing smile swiftly fades at

The mention of your name-

It's a shame.

Have you ever seen her when she is

overjoyed?

She is a silly picture of girlish beauty.

Find a way to get back into her heart.

Climb the hills, walk through the valleys,

Negotiate the thorns to get to your rose.

She is worth it.

She often mimics toughness,

But her vulnerability shines through,

I see her need for you.

It's not too late f-a-t-h-e-r.

There is still time.

Mend the torn pieces,

Reduce the distance,

Make your way back into her sweetheart.

She still has space to welcome you home.

Yours truly,

Her "school daddy".

Touched (for that young girl)

r. A. bentinck

After a while

I sensed something wasn't right.

She was so blessed with natural beauty

But she couldn't see it from

Behind stained eyes.

Somedays she carried herself

Like a dirty rag doll,

On other days she was

The excited princess with

A skip in her steps and

Sparkles in her eyes.

I worried in silence

And enquired with cautious

But probing questions.

She was always guarded.

Her answers kept me at

Arm's length.

A multiplicity of

Fluctuating emotions and

And contrasting personalities

Always give me sneak peeks

But never enough to form a

Concrete conclusion.

Then one day…

One day

She musters up the courage to

Summoned me to an impromptu meeting.

And she told me her story.

"He TOUCHED me

INAPPROPRIATELY."

Her eyes were glazed with

That familiar dreary look.

That always concerned me.

"He stole my innocence,

I am no longer pure!"

Her voice was tainted

With hurt and regret.

"He touched me!"

It was always her dream to

Save herself for that special someone.

She wanted to savour those first

Moments:

Her first butterfly moments,

Her first kiss,

Her first moments of amorous bliss.

"He stole it all from me!"

Her trust in boys and meaningful

Relationships have been destroyed.

Her ability to see her

Her natural beauty objectively

Is SHATTERED!

All because he

Touched her inappropriately.

Daughters
(for Michael and Francis)

r. A. bentinck

As sisters,

You sense that sturdy bond

That fashioned them

Into inseparable siblings.

They have endured

Many rocky roads together.

They have in plentitude

Those qualities that would

Make any father recognise

Over time,

That they were

Heaven-sent.

They are extraordinary

Blessings to any parents.

They can be

Stressful

And

Stress-filled

But

Mostly they are affectionate princesses.

They are teenage queens

Who's company and friendship

Have unfolded on me

Over the years.

They are my 30 Carat Pink Diamond.

They have filled my island life

With distinctive and

Imperishable memories.

Unassuming Beauty (for Kimberly)

r. A. bentinck

Her loveliness is like

Still waters,

It runs deep.

She doesn't often smile

But when she does

It's like the newborn sun;

Uplifting,

Warm,

Inviting,

Dazzling and rejuvenating.

Her eyes tell a thousand

Oriental tales

And reflects the quintessence

Of her gentle soul.

Her cleverness embodies

The stuff of Chinese Proverbs

And speaks to the wisdom

Beyond her years.

Her presence adds serenity to

Chaotic environments.

She does everything with

Unassuming ease,

She is that kind of beautiful.

Her First Day of School

r. A. bentinck

She was a chatty bundle of excitement

As we walked her to school

This is the day she was looking forward to,

She spent countless hours at home

Walking around in her uniform and her

lunch kit.

On the way to school,

She skipped,

She hopped,

She jumped.

She was a picture of joy.

Then we entered the school gate

And she changed from a princess to a Frog.

Her skippy steps became stuttered.

She was dead quiet.

The smile on her face was replaced

With a perplexed mask.

This wasn't my daughter.

Her hands became tense

When she heard the cries seeping through

The distant classroom windows.

A gorgeous teacher with

A charming smile greeted us.

The introductory formalities

Seem to pass in the nick of time.

She looked so pretty in her uniform

But her face was contorted with distress.

I stooped down to kiss her goodbye, and

Her tiny hands swiftly wrapped around my

neck

In a deadly hug.

I felt like a helpless lamb

In the powerful squeeze of

A vicious anaconda.

I struggled to break free and

Her hug got tighter and stronger.

After a prolong and intense struggle

With the aid of the teacher,

I managed to escape.

I walked away slowly,

Physically exhausted and mentally

wounded.

My heart began to bleed

As she joined the bawling orchestra

Of children singing a symphony of sorrow.

She quickly became the lead vocalist.

I could hear her to the pinnacle of

Her lungs screaming,

"DADDY, DADDY, DADDY!"

Her screams changed to please,

And her pleas to sustained squeals.

Soon her squealing notes overpowered

Her fragile vocal cords and her voice

Started to crack.

She began to choke on her daddy calls.

As I disappeared into the distance

Her calls faded,

But I was still a broken father

On her first day of school.

She Calls Me Father (for Delicia)

r. A. bentinck

She crept into my heart one day.

And from then on,

Day by day,

Week by week,

Month by month,

Year by year,

She built a place of comfort.

She fostered and nurtured my

Fatherly qualities,

She made loving her unconditionally,

Effortless.

She moulded a sacred place in my heart and

Made it her home.

Then one day she started calling me father.

She is comely.

She is gentle yet feisty,

She is caring and loving,

She is simple yet complicated,

She is gifted and blessed.

In my heart, she has fashioned a place to

stay.

I'm not sure she knows how much

She dominates this space.

Over time she has

Grown to love me,

To trust my counsel,

And to lean on me.

This little girl who one day

Crept into my heart

Has now created a permanent place to abide.

With You (for King)

Ackeeni Bentinck

With you,

It was not love at first sight

For we didn't see eye to eye

We both had 'Xs' and 'Ys.'

We both had problems

But I solved yours, and you solved mine

Forming the perfect simultaneous equation

With you,

Falling in Love was no fairytale.

There was no rescuing of a princess

Or breaking of spells from true love's kiss

But there were fire, passion and bliss.

With you,

Being perfect was overrated,

For we basked in our imperfections.

We both were beautifully flawed

In our unique way

And fell in love with

each other without dismay

With You,

I finally felt loved

Knowing that there was someone

Who wanted and needed me

Someone who respected and cherished me.

That's how I knew,

From that very instance,

That I wanted to be with you.

Dear Baby

Ackeeni Bentinck

Dear baby,

At the moment you are just

A combination of mommy and daddy's

DNA

Which are cells that will form tissues

And the miraculous process will go on and

on

Until having ten perfect fingers and toes

A cute little button nose

Big eyes like your mommy

And your daddy's face.

Dear baby,

As you grow and become noticeable

Many harsh critics will come

To tarnish mommy's character

And may try to convince mommy

To be a patient in the 'slip and fell' Ward

But I promise you that I will be strong

And I will keep you safe from all harm

Because I rather they speak ill of me

Than about you.

Dear baby,

Know that mommy and daddy love you

With all our hearts and soul

And that we relish in the thought of

Your presence though you were not planned

Know that is not and will never be a mistake

But an unexpected blessing to us both.

Dear baby,

Mommy and daddy are excited to meet you.

Letter to Daddy

Ackeeni Bentinck

Dear daddy,

I remember waiting for you

In a lilac and purple-flowered dress

That I carefully picked out

Knowing that when you saw me in it,

You will call me beautiful,

And I will blush my face off

For I yearned for your compliment

After a long week of insults and harsh

criticism

I remember standing on the verandah

Awaiting your arrival as you promised.

I waited and waited in the scorching

afternoon sun

For what seemed like hours,

With searching eyes piercing into

Every vehicle that stopped

Hoping that you will step out of one.

I stood there until dusk

Until the stars were my only confidant

Though it was clear that you weren't

coming,

I still waited and hoped.

But my optimism weaken

And my heart shattered into a million pieces

And my brain immediately started to

Pick up the pieces and instead of tears,

I began to ache on the inside.

My brain, still trying the assemble

The pieces of my heart,

Failed to transmit the message to my tear

ducts

That it was ok to cry

I couldn't cry. Instead, I became choked up

 With anger, betrayal and bitterness

And unto this very day

 I still don't know the reason why

You didn't show up.

Was it something I said?

Was it something I did?

Tell me why have neglected me?

Should I conclude,

That you didn't want me too?

She is My Girl (for Ackeeni)

r. A. bentinck

When I first laid eyes on her

I was a picture of disarrayed excitement.

After nine months there she was,

A bundle of unspeakable bliss.

She is my girl.

She converted me into her bed,

And my chest became her favourite pillow

And dribbling receptacle.

She is my girl.

I became a master at changing and washing

Dirty diapers.

I won her bedtime story laureate

A thousand times over.

She is my girl.

 She changed my name to Daddy,

Convinced me to become a donkey, a lion,

And a monkey

And then tells me how much she loves me.

She is my girl.

I blinked, now am left wondering…

"Where did the years go?"

She traded in her favourite rag teddy bear

For a boy.

Now am hearing whispering hints of

Marriage and a family.

She is still my girl,

And she still calls me daddy.

About the Authors

Randy Abubakar Bentinck

r. A. bentinck is an emerging writer who is a

graduate of the University of Guyana and

the Burrowes School of Art. His work explores themes of love, loss, relationship, social issues and femininity, he writes from a deeply personal place, but his work is still relatable.

Bentinck first published a book of poems is called "Of all the Lilies". He was very active in the theatre scene in Guyana during the 90s where he acted in many major productions at the Theatre Guild of Guyana and the National Cultural Center.

As a visual artist, he has been a part of several national exhibitions, and his work represented Guyana at Carifesta IX, held in Trinidad and Tobago in 2006.

He has been very active in sports and youth development. He was the chaperone for a youth contingent from Guyana for the first Habitat For Humanity Caribbean Youth Build held in 2000.

For more work from r. A. bentinck, please visit his website: www.randybentinck.com.

My Girl

Ackeeni Qwanza Ngozi Bentinck

Though a teacher by profession, Ackeeni
Bentinck always had a passion poetry.
Bentinck uses poetry to express her inner
thoughts, address social issues and to be the

voice for the voiceless. She was born and raised in the garden city of Georgetown in Guyana. She attended the North Ruimveldt Multilateral Secondary and graduated in 2011. In September of that same year, she started college at the Cyril Potter's College of Education and graduated as a trained teacher with an Associate Degree in Education. She is presently a teacher at a Senior Secondary in the heart of Georgetown. Apart from teaching and poetry, Bentinck loves to take part in drama and dance. She wrote a number of plays, one being 'Faithful are the Wounds of a Friend." which made it to the finals at the National Drama Festival 2016. Also, she graduated with a diploma from the National School of

Theatre Arts and Drama in the year 2016. Bentinck is also currently pursuing her Bachelor's Degree in Education at the University of Guyana. She is both introvert and extrovert. She loves to go out and have fun, but at the same time values those moments which she spends alone in the tranquillity of her home.